When a Child
Dies From Drugs

.

When a Child Dies From Drugs

Practical Help for Parents in Bereavement

Patricia Wittberger
&
Russ Wittberger

To order additional copies of this book, contact:
Xlibris Corporation
1-888-795-4274
www.Xlibris.com
Orders@Xlibris.com
22187

Contents

We dedicate this volume to all those who have left this earthly life through the misuse of drugs or alcohol, to the parents, brothers, sisters and others who remain here to love them, miss them and always have them in their hearts.

ACKNOWLEDGMENTS

First we need to thank our daughter, Jennifer Caroline, for being a part of our lives yesterday, today and forever.

Second, Pat wishes to thank Russ most gratefully for his steadfast support both as a true partner in all that conveys and for giving up tempting thoughts of retirement to finance the creations of "Jenny's Journey" and GRASP ("Grief Recovery After a Substance Passing"), plus all other efforts to reach out wherever needed. Truly a guardian angel.

To our five other children: Steven, Rob, Elizabeth, Gary and Scott, who have traveled much of our paths with us. We love you all.

Thanks, also, to the unknown authors of "Please" and "In The Silence." We searched diligently for you because many have been touched by your words and we use them here to reach out once again.

Lastly, to all those persons who have encouraged, pushed, suggested and had faith in us, especially our mothers from GRASP, thank you for your sharing and friendship whether through personal contacts or otherwise.

Thanks to each and every one of you. May you always have an angel at your side.

PREFACE

After the initial shock of being told of, and accepting, our daughter's death from heroin, we sought to contact an understanding grieving group to advise and aid us through these numbing disoriented times.

We began with the telephone directory and phoned a couple of groups. Their replies were discouraging. From funeral directors and clergy came platitudes that slid over the surface of our particular needs.

Were we, then, the *only* parents in San Diego city or county, to ever lose a child this way? How about California or the entire country?

We searched library and bookstore shelves for a book that would point us on the way to understanding what was happening to us in the tumultuous aftermath of our child's death due to drug misuse.

There were many volumes addressing bereavement. No doubt they were excellent but none dealt specifically with substances and our torments.

Death at any time is traumatic, to say the least. A *child's* death, regardless of age, is even more so.

The majority of deaths we can understand, although it doesn't make the heartache any less for families, especially parents. Miscarriage, stillbirth and crib deaths are tragically accepted as occurring from "natural causes" through no one's actions or faults.

Illness is treated by medication, physician and hospital

guidance, and when death results there is the acceptance of having rendered all possible aid.

The absolute sudden finality of life due to accidents or murder is extremely difficult for a family to assimilate.

All the above need, demand and receive immediate sympathy and caring, *as they should.*

But what of the children, from teenage through adulthood, who leave this earth because of addictions to drugs, alcohol and other substances?

This is a death whispered about. Was it suicide? Accidental? What sort of person is this? What sort of parents allow this?

Chances are that these parents have sought advice and fought battles with and for their children's lives for years before this tragic demise. They have also done everything in their power to help the child.

How are they greeted? No one rushes to tell them that their broken hearts will mend or how to react to the tumble of emotions being experienced, including severe guilt. They hurt when people step away at the news. Is this OK? Some say "sorry" and quickly absent themselves.

This death is shocking.

This death is a disgrace.

Do not speak of it.

We had nothing about which to be secretive. We announced the *truth* about our daughter's death to friends and acquaintances and urged her siblings to do likewise. To do otherwise would have been unthinkable.

You feel as though you are the only family in the universe to have had such a death occur. Yet, logic tells you this is ridiculous. Why won't someone tell me that I am feeling as I am supposed to feel? Please someone, step forward to help sort out my emotions at this time.

Yes, we decided to write this book after hearing from other parents of their search for literature, anything to address their needs in this circumstance. We sincerely hope that "When a Child Dies From Drugs" will help to answer questions, aid in taking steps forward and, most of all, be comforted in the knowledge of *not* being *alone* on the planet. So often friends would like to offer aid but are hesitant, not quite knowing what to say. Answers to this, also, are here.

As mentioned in the first paragraph, our child, our daughter Jennifer's death resulted from a heroin overdose. Jennifer was three months short of her twenty-first birthday. She had tried to overcome her addictions for the previous five years. Addiction was not her career choice. On the evening of her death she was preparing, in the next days, to enter a treatment facility, determined to have a new life. Heroin. One last injection. We lost one more lovely, gifted, highly intelligent young soul who forever leaves a void in her parents' hearts.

Even one child's passing due to substances is too many, but as long as they're happening, we, the parents who have to survive, finding a way through the mazes of agonizingly missing them, must reach out in sharing and caring for one another.

When grief first strikes, everything is perceived as though you are in a darkened room. Everything outside and beyond your present challenges and emotions does not exist.

Then you realize that if you raise up the shades and let in even a sliver of light, you become more aware of your immediate surroundings and the room itself.

Slowly lifting up the shades, a few inches at a time, you see that the light begins to illuminate the entire room.

Then, when you fully open the shade and let the sun stream through, you become aware of all there is outside. Everything that was there before you entered the darkness is still there, waiting for you.

So it is with grief. In our devastation, we can only be aware of the immediate needs, the demanding pressures and pain of the present.

Eventually . . .

You will lift up the shades and step out of your darkness.

Why "Dear Friend" to begin some of the chapters? Because we think of all who telephone, email, write or meet with us to share their troubled but wonderful children, as our friends. We come to you through these pages as concerned, loving friends who we would comfort with an embrace if we could. As you approach the book's conclusion we would want you to feel the same kinship.

May you always have an angel beside you.

Pat and Russ Wittberger

INTRODUCTION

Dear Friend:

There is no doubt about it. You have received the worst possible news that a parent can learn. Your child has left this earth—has died from the misuse of drugs. No "good-bye."

Your child. That gurgling baby, that busy, happy toddler. That questioning six year-old. The troubled teen. Gone. Too soon. Too young.

The child that you cared for through illness, healed scrapes with a kiss or band-aid or both. Passed on. Dead.

No matter how this tragic news was relayed, whether from the lips of a policeman or woman at the door or a telephone call from some other authority or a hospital, there is no way we are supposed to hear those words telling us that a precious life—our child's life—has ended.

As parents, we are not handed an instruction booklet as we welcome our children into the world. Wouldn't that be wonderful? Then there would be no more fumbling and guessing and trying to figure out if we were doing the correct thing for this complicated creature who has been entrusted to our care.

Those baby-eyes and child's eyes look trustingly at us. They know we will care for their every need. As new parents we feel somewhat inadequate, nervous and, although we become more comfortable in our role, we never truly lose that little bit of "scariness" at this responsibility.

Just as we are not handed the instruction book of life, neither are we told what to do about the last chapter of it—death.

No-one discusses death. No-one mentions death except pre-emptably. And, certainly, not in the context of our children.

In the order of all things, all cycles, we are born, we live and we die, but always the elders leave first, don't they? It will be for our children to make decisions for our death. Not the other way around.

This cannot be.

PRONOUNCEMENT

Dear Friend:

I am sorry. I am so sincerely sorry that this tragedy has happened to you.

When you heard that pronouncement, your world was shattered in one instant. Perhaps you even lost consciousness, a merciful blotting out of the senses for a brief moment. Or perhaps your mind denied the possibility of this horrendous happening before switching to a numbing *autopilot* of reflexes.

Who is that crying out—a howling like a wounded animal?

No one ever told us of the real, physical pain that can strike at the stomach, the solar plexus. The heart really does *break* with pain.

Your very soul wants to reach out and cradle this lost one who is gone from us.

The pain is unbearable.

And yet, it is to be borne, to be endured.

Friend, you are not alone. Please remember this fact. There are many, many of us across countries and continents who have been or are now bearing similar anguish.

CHAPTER 1

ALONE

Yet, you do feel isolated. All alone. An island.
Even with a spouse in as much pain.
Even with other children near.
Even with other family members.
Even with one friend or a circle.

**No-one feels exactly the same physical or mental anguish
as the next individual.**

This is part of our uniqueness. We each move in our own
space and time. We each feel emotions *as* deeply but not always
in synchronicity with one another.

There are times when it will be good to be alone, to release
the deep sobs that will be dredged from the bottom of your being.
At this moment, you are not ready to seek.

When someone offers consoling arms, accept them and let
your tears flow.

CHAPTER 2

DENIAL

There is an unreality to all that has happened and continues to unfold.

This most traumatic of tragedies has happened, possibly preceded by weeks, months or even years of emotional heart-breaking turmoil, when you have searched, loved and tried to understand and help your special person.

In the far recesses of your mind there may have lurked the thought that, yes, a call could come one day to say that your troubled child had died.

But we never *really* expected it to happen to us—to *our* child. It will only happen to *them*—those other people. Too bad for them. But *we* will be the fortunate ones who will battle through addictions and emerge victorious.

Perhaps, when the pronouncement tore at the very core of your being, there was an even greater impact, because your child had never been lured by drugs? So how could this be? There were no signs. No addictons. No conflict within the family over school or friends.

Yet, death, in the guise of a substance, had reached out to claim another young life.

This cannot be

This is not true.

This is not happening. This needs to be rejected.

When our daughter died, my mind needed to have the statement repeated over and over like a mantra to be imprinted on the brain.

"My daughter is dead."

"JC has died."

For the first two days this was played continuously while my body functioned automatically and dealt with the breathing, walking, and decision-making we wanted to ignore.

Some people cannot even *say* the words "death," "dead," "died," for weeks or months afterward. They are words of finality.

We do not want to be final—to be finished with this person.

There is nothing wrong in using other phrases, even though there are experts who would argue against our belief. "Passing on." "Gone." "Lost." These are the preferences of many.

We understand perfectly well that the vibrant personalities we love are no longer physically with us. They haven't gone into their room or on a trip, and they're not lost, as in missing. But, in order to *begin* an acceptance, our minds and heartache need to have a little comfort this way, especially in the first days when this whole tragedy must sink in and we need gentleness.

We surely were not meant to sit across the table from a stranger to discuss funeral arrangements for our child.

CHAPTER 3

ACCEPTANCE

The most difficult fact to accept in these circumstances is that your child is no longer with us.

For those parents who do not have the opportunity, whether through distance or time, to identify or see their child, it must be even harder for you to rely on another's information.

Even when, as in our case, a sibling was with our daughter as she was rushed to hospital, I had to have *proof* of her death.

Death occurred in another city and even through making arrangements and decisions, acceptance wasn't fully there until I actually viewed her lifeless form.

But, my friend, this is only the beginning of truly accepting and it may be over the course of several months that you acknowledge this entire episode has not been someone's idea of a macabre joke.

Within the first months there is the longing to hear their voice over the telephone.

To have them walk into a room.

To hold them.

Slowly, week-by-week, month-by-month, we accept that this is not going to happen.

Oh, we miss these creatures so very much. But we accept the challenge to continue our lives even with an emptiness inside that was their place.

Acceptance of a child no longer being on earth does not mean that we forget them.

On the contrary it can be absolutely the opposite.

You will always have their image in your head. A happy image.

You will always have many memories. Happy memories.

You will always love them.

You will always have their love for you.

For these are our very special people who also came into our lives to be cherished and will have left us with some special gifts of learning.

Eventually you will discover that you will learn more about living through their death.

Cherish others.

Cherish moments.

Cherish love.

With growing *acceptance* of this situation in which we find ourselves, we can move forward, *forward* day by day.

Your Thoughts

"Pain"

"Your pain is the breaking of the shell that encloses
your understanding."

"The Prophet:" Kahlil Gibran

CHAPTER 4

TEARS & HEALING

Dear Friend:

Cry. Let your tears flow to help ease the ache in your soul. Do not be afraid of the sobs that will wrack your body through their depth.

You are hurting and tears help with our healing.

Do not try to dam the flood—your body knows better than your intellect what is good for you.

What *if* you cry each time you tell someone of your child's death?

You have the best reason in this world to cry.

They may need to turn away or they may simply put an arm around you.

It could take several months before you can say something without a tear.

That's ok. . . . *You* are ok.

Do not be surprised:

If tears trickle down when hearing a favorite piece of music.

If you see something in a store that they would have liked.

If you catch sight of someone who resembles them.

If you are in a store and realize you are going to be overwhelmed with emotion, simply walk out to your car and sit there while you cry. Do *not* drive in this state. It is quite all right to leave the groceries or other shopping when you need to do this.

Quite often we cry in our sleep, especially when we have dreamed of being with our loved one. This is acceptable, too. There is nothing unnatural about this.

In all probability you are going to continue crying easily throughout the first year or two and feel better for it! Eventually the occurrences will lessen but not completely disappear.

Not so surprisingly, there will be gentle tears when the joy of a shared memory surfaces, to be held close for a moment to help heal your heart.

CHAPTER 5

GUILT & BLAME

When a child dies because of drugs, whether or not there was addiction involved, one of the most difficult emotions to come to terms with is *guilt*.

Because of guilt, many deny that their child had any problems in this area, especially if they have kept struggles secret from family and friends.

When a death occurs, overdoses are often masked as: "It was so sudden, but he/she has been ill for some time . . . a blood disorder . . . a mystery sickness." Or even, "an accident."

Because all the above are acceptable to society.

Regardless of how many years you have spent in nightmare scenarios of battles with and for this child, ever seeking treatments and advice, the addiction hell that can change a home into a constant war zone means a guilty verdict for parents when the child succumbs.

Why? You have tried. You have failed.

You are not society's "perfect" parents or you would have been successful.

You are guilty of allowing your child to become an addict.

You are guilty of allowing your child to die.

And you see guilt thrust upon you by others when you speak out the truth and ask that they recall the "real" person they knew before the drugs took control. The sometime physical distancing between you. Eyes that grow cold and unsmiling. The mumbled "sorry" or just "oh" as they hurry away and get on with their lives.

They do not know what to say or how to re-act. A clasp of hands in genuine warmth would suffice.

You can almost hear their sighs of "Thank goodness *my* child is perfect and wouldn't dream of that!"

I pray for them that their child remains so.

Continue to tell the truth about your child.

Family and friends know the real person.

You must shed your guilt by affirming that you all did your utmost against an overpowering enemy.

Keep that truth close to your heart. *You did your best.*

Because of this confusing guilt, we begin to look at the previous days, weeks or months before this death.

Parents may find it so easy to accuse one another of neglect at this time. A time of "who shouldered the most burden," etc. A weak marriage can fall apart because of blame. Even siblings share in this game as they become aware of what they may or may not have done to help.

You must try to put everything into perspective.

It was your child's choice.

Your Thoughts

CHAPTER 6

WHAT-IFS & SUPPOSES?

Dear Friend:

Have you gone down the "what-ifs" road yet?

The "what-ifs" follow closely on the heels of the guilt trips we thrust upon ourselves.

You know what I mean.

"What if I had locked him/her in the bedroom that night (or day)?"

"What if I'd been more vigilant in the very beginning?"

"What if we'd tried path number ten instead of number six? Or we'd tried number ten *and* number six?"

And the "supposes:"

"Suppose he/she had chosen not to befriend that person or been persuaded to . . ."

"Suppose we had all tried every possible preventative measure available to us, would the outcome have been any different?"

The debilitating What-Ifs and the Supposes. You can take your mind in circles by going in this direction.

Please don't.

Nothing can alter what has occurred. Because "what if" you had been able to change the course of one day or week, perhaps this nightmare scenario may have played out the same way after all.

We don't know. We'll never know. It must simply be accepted and let the questions go.

Take a deep breath.

Let us move forward now.

CHAPTER 7

ANGER & FORGIVENESS

In the midst of your emotional roller coaster ride of these first weeks and months, don't be surprised to discover, somewhere between the achingly painful "missing them," the guilt trips and what-ifs, that you also feel *anger* rising to the surface.

Anger at what? "At whom?" do you ask.

At the person or *persons* who supplied the fatal poison, is an obvious first choice.

But there are other reasons to be angry.

Self. How could I have *not* prevented this passing? Why was I so stupidly blind in the very beginning? Why didn't I recognize "the signs"?

Spouse. Where was the needed support—in the beginning? Anytime? Where was the intervention when chaos threatened?

Children. Other family members. Can't they respond to the pain you are experiencing? Why aren't they more sympathetic? Can't they see that you are falling apart—that the world has crumbled?

God. Why was your child ignored? You had incessantly prayed for them to be watched over, to be helped, to be "saved." How could the All Mighty, Spirit, Entity, ignore your pleas?

Your child. How *dare* they do this to you after all you had been through and weathered together? How could they be so foolish?

It helps to be alone to yell aloud at each of these. To rage and storm and cry impassioned tears until exhaustion overcomes your body.

It eases these feelings to admit to your spouse that anger toward them has been in your mind. But—*and this is important*—not while you are in a "simmering" mode. Only at a time of communicating on a confiding, quiet level. You may be surprised to learn that they, too, have had similar thoughts, which need to be faced and dealt with.

With children and other family members, also try to explain to them why you have felt their indifference toward you, even after a lapse of several weeks after the event. Perhaps they were also so deeply distressed that they didn't know *how* to respond to their own grief as well as yours.

Of course, you cannot confront your child to be answered but you can speak aloud to them (using a photograph helps) and vent your thoughts. Who knows, perhaps they are nearby and can hear and see us and may be waiting for your forgiveness?

For *forgiveness* does follow anger, eventually.

This is one of the most difficult parts in healing.

Begin with *yourself*. Knowing that you have done all in your capacity as a parent to nurture, guide and care for this child. A stage is reached in every individual's life when nothing more can be done as a caregiver and you must relinquish that role.

Forgive yourself.

Your child. No matter what circumstances brought them to this situation—peer pressure, temperament, opportunity—the choice was ultimately theirs. It was the wrong choice. Be sorry for their choice. Forgive their mistake. Remember only their love.

My friend, I found it most difficult to forgive the person who had set our daughter onto the slippery slope of addiction. It took more than two years before I was not upset by thoughts of their continued life while my loved one had departed the earth plane. I meditated and prayed to know forgiveness for them. Little by little, it was peaceful within my heart.

As for God, I also arrived at the realization that my child *had* been cared for and spared any further pain, although this, too, took a long time for acceptance, because even as I told myself or heard from other lips that "she is in a better place," I denied that vehemently because I needed her in *my* arms and in *my* place!

Your Thoughts

CHAPTER 8

A MOTHER'S THOUGHTS

Dear Friend:

Understanding and coming to terms with that roller coaster ride of emotions we experience is not easily accomplished and we are confronted, or even jolted, with a sometimes peculiarly maternal thought.

Within a short space of time after hearing of our daughter's passing, and even within the first pain of grief, a "wave" of relief washed over and through me. "It is over," came the phrase. For her, all the hurt, the battles with addictions, were finished. I felt "good" for *her* sake. Then almost immediately I was engulfed with the present agony.

Some days later the realization came, "Who do I worry about now?" "What do I worry about now?"

After so much of life centered around this person—what now? An empty chasm.

I knew that *eventually* I would fill that chasm, although the "how" was as yet an unknown quantity.

The lying awake at night wondering where they are, who they're with? Are they safe? Praying that someone watch over them.

That is over now.

Waiting for a phone call, to hear their voice. To know they are alive.

That is gone.

And even as we grapple with the realities of this death in the first days, our nurturing instincts rise to the fore with the thoughts of:

"I hope she's warm enough. I hope they've covered her with a blanket."

We think of this as so irrational and yet, I have heard other mothers express the same or similar sentiments.

And then the *longing* begins quite soon.

Needing to know, just as in their earth journey, that they are OK. If they could only call.

Wanting to hear their voice when the telephone rings.

"It's a mistake!"

A "joke" perpetrated by a "friend."

Longing . . .

To have them be at the door when the buzzer sounds, or to burst in with news.

Longing . . .

And you are helpless and empty once more and your arms ache to hold them. To feel them. To smell them. To kiss them. To love them.

And (here comes an "if-only") we would like to be able to *bargain.*

Anything—even the hell you have already experienced trying to help them—is preferable to the pain that is felt now.

You would give your life to give them another chance.

And we are as helpless in our sorrow as they were helpless in their battles.

Your Thoughts

CHAPTER 9

A FATHER'S POINT OF VIEW

It's no secret that men are far different from women—*emotionally* as well as physically.

But in the event of losing a child through drugs, the pain is so unreal, so devastating that, in order for a marriage to survive, the man and wife operate in unison to get through the horrible ordeals facing them during that nightmarish first day, first week, and first month.

This is not something you practice for. There are no "manuals" that mean anything to *you* when the worst thing in life happens.

You do everything as you go, make decisions you've never had to remotely consider before. More than at any time of crisis in a couple's lives, they must now somehow work together for each other, handling the hour-by-hour challenges that neither of them has ever faced before.

As that first anguished week passes by, and you somehow survive, the inevitable question surfaces: Whose fault was it? The husband's? The wife's? While neither party may say it in words, it's only natural for each to consciously decide who was to blame.

In most cases, the true answer is likely to be: *Both* or *neither.* Surely if a couple has made all reasonable efforts to avert the tragedy (whether they will agree with that or not), this was a circumstance that could have been likely to happen anytime.

Next month? Next year? There is a limit to what the most caring couple in the world can do.

But if one spouse feels strongly that the *other* is at fault, the marriage is often on a course for breakup.

The guilt and grief is intensive enough, just having to have lost a beloved child. But if one spouse feels they were the significant cause of the death, the guilt may be too much to bear, without the support of their mate. Eventually other issues in the marriage surface, and often separation or divorce is the only way for both parties to survive.

The basic roles of men and women in the nurturing and development of a child are obviously *enormously* different.

It's the woman who goes through the nine-month span of bearing the child and then goes through the birth process. Men have no real way to understand the physical hell that accompanies child bearing. (Carole Burnett said that for a man to fully comprehend what it feels like to give birth, he needs to "take his lower lip and pull it up and over his eyebrows.")

The real differences between men and women in the life of a child rest in the roles they have in most cases been given.

The man's traditional duty, we're told, is to provide for the welfare of his family. He must provide shelter, food and warmth for them. The caveman, traditionally, went out to catch game, and probably risked his life in the process. If he was not successful, his family would starve, so he somehow prevailed. All the while, the women stayed at home with the children, protecting and nurturing them, awaiting the Big Hunter's return.

Simplified, of course. But as life moves on, the woman tends to be the one who spends more time with the child—shopping for clothes, talking over their problems, getting them dressed and fed for school, chauffeuring them to after school events and, when necessary, wiping their noses.

Meanwhile, the man is out each day hunting down a large grizzly bear for supper (i.e., earning a living, to provide for his wife and children).

The point is that, even in the cases of both spouses working, the woman, beginning with the birth of the child, is likely to be more physically and emotionally in touch with the young one on a continuing basis, than the man.

So the potential for guilt on the part of *both* spouses is enormous, for the husband ("I wasn't *there* for her. It was my fault.") and for the wife ("I was there, but I wasn't able to turn her around. It was my fault.")

Guilt can be more destructive than any gun or knife. Eventually those marriages that survive face the fact that no matter who was at fault, if anyone, partners need to get by that and move on.

Men are supposed to suppress their tears more than women. I don't know where that stuff came from. Probably from the Big Grizzly Bear Syndrome mentioned previously. Forget that. I cried then, even in public, and even more when in the company of my wife. I don't recall that I cried much, or at all, prior to Jenny.

When I was ten and living in St. Paul, Minnesota, I was standing on a street corner one frigid January afternoon, chatting with my best friend, Tom Rosene. Kids were throwing snowballs at each other in wintry fun. But someone somewhere had made a perfect ice ball and hurled it at us while we weren't looking. It crashed into my forehead with such force that I fell to my knees. I started crying, just for a half minute.

When the ice was brushed away, Tom said: "Russ, that was the first time I ever saw you cry. I didn't know that you could cry."

I remember feeling humiliated because I had cried in public, in front of my best buddy. I had been well indoctrinated even at ten: Boys aren't allowed to cry.

I pretty much followed that tradition, until Jenny died.

Sadly, in many quarters men today are still not considered *real* men if they cry. But where loss of life is concerned, and especially the kind of tragedy addressed here, tears are an important way to make it through the agonizing realities we face.

I remember my first day "back in public," about a week after the funeral, feeling I was okay to go back to work. I was driving along the freeway in San Diego, feeling emotionally secure. But when I saw the outlines of my office building in the distance, I couldn't do it. I tightly grasped the wheel and drove right by the exit ramp. A mile later I stopped in a Denny's parking lot, and cried again.

I realized I wasn't strong enough to go to work that day, so I stepped inside the restaurant and ordered a cup of coffee. Maybe if I wait a while, I'll be okay. But a funny thing happened. As I looked at the people at their tables, talking, laughing, I found myself thinking: "What are you people doing?? Don't you realize my daughter is dead?? How can you possibly be happy??"

I knew I was not yet ready to drift back into society, and I went home for that day.

I cried most of the way home.

It got better, of course. As the weeks, the months, and then years went by, it was seldom that I found myself in tears. Yet, I miss Jenny as badly right this minute than I did that first day.

To those who have suffered this unimaginable loss recently, I can tell you it *will* get better. Sometime. You will find that you exist for longer periods—a minute, a day?—when you don't have the thought of that precious loss taking over your mind.

If you are to survive, you must get beyond grief, beyond guilt, behind the regrets (the "if onlys" and "what ifs") and move on. No, it's not easy. But it's not impossible.

This does not mean that you will in any way be disrespectful of the memory of your departed loved one. Not at all. I think they *expect* us to move on. You will somehow find yourself remembering the *good* times you had, instead of those tragic moments that seared your mind so forcefully during the first year.

I often think about how I made the transition from being totally devastated and almost incapable of functioning, at many times during that first year after Jenny's passing, to just *living my life a day at a time.*

Time enters into this, but only a little. In my case, the first year was by far the most traumatic. I found that by throwing myself into work, or meaningful outside activities, I was able to break the sieges of sadness.

The most important point is that, in order to get by and maintain your life following the loss of a child through drugs, you must have help. It's hard to survive on your own.

Yet some of the logical sources for support may not readily be there. To a great degree, your close friends, relatives and fellow workers hesitate to even bring up the name of your lost child. They feel it will be hurtful to you. To be frank, most do not have an idea of just how to talk about the subject of death through drugs with you, and isn't that understandable? Unless you've *been there,* no one can be truly compassionate to your pain. So where to turn?

The first source is your mate. The two of you have so much *common hurt* that talking it out, leaning on each other, will help in surviving the ordeal—from day one to year ten.

But, to be sure, the person who has lost a child through the misuse of drugs will never be the same, will never be fully free of the flashing thoughts, the down days, and the visions of what might have been. That will be a part of your being, so live for the better days, and spend more time focusing on all the *good* things that were a part of your life with that child.

My mind often drifts back to Jenny as a little girl, when everything was so rosy, so full of promise. Laughter and love were constant companions.

I remember one Saturday morning, as I drove three year old Jenny to my office to "help with my paperwork," as I often did. We were driving along Mission Gorge Road in San Diego and were approaching a towering mountain range to our left.

"Daddy, you know what?" Jenny said softly.

"No. What?"

Pause. "I bet that mountain has been here since before you were born," she said.

I looked over at her, smiling and impressed with how smart she was. "You're probably right, Jenny."

Five minutes later she said, "And I bet it was there even before gramma and grampa were born."

I agreed again.

As we approached my office, the mountain range long faded behind us, she said:

"And you know what, daddy? I bet it'll *still* be there after all of us are gone."

When I think of that story, I always realize that she had it exactly right. We're here to enjoy today, as best we can, and when we eventually move on, the mountain will still be there.

And so will Jenny.

Your Thoughts

CHAPTER 10

PROMISES #1

I do not have a magic wand to wave over you, my friend. I wish I had that plus words to eliminate your pain in this tragedy.

What I *do* have are suggestions for you. Discoveries of my own and others to ease your suffering and enable you to begin to recover from your grief.

All will happen in *your own time.*

I *promise* you that eventually the physical pain will lessen and become an occasional hurt.

You will smile more.

You will laugh.

There will be gentle tears, not a flood.

That time will pass and days go by.

That you will heal into a peaceful time.

That you will learn.

That you will love.

CHAPTER 11

THINGS TO DO—
THE NEXT STEP FORWARD

Dear Friend:

Some of the things that I am going to tell you will sound so simple but I know that they work and hope they help you in whatever way you need to be aided at this time.

Of course, I cannot know your opinion on what happens after death but I am sure this is one thought that surfaces frequently.

Personally, I knew that our daughter believed in a continuation of a life force after death, as do my husband and I. This did not mean that we would not grieve or miss her any less intensely but we *eventually* were somewhat comforted by this philosophy.

From the first day after learning of her passing, I talked to her aloud—usually looking at a photograph and then, more frequently, simply as part of an on-going dialogue.

1. *Talk to your precious angel.*

2. *Talk about them.* There is a great need to bring them into daily conversation. Do that. When you feel that your family has heard enough, discover a friend who'll share remembrances with you. A bereavement group

for listening to one another and share their "real" person, *not* the one in addiction, can be vital.

3. *Make the effort.* There are days when you may feel that you just don't want to face the world—to stay huddled beneath a blanket. To get out of bed requires a great effort of energy. *Make that effort.* Continue to move into your routine of showering, eating. You don't have to hold long conversations with other people.

4. *Sleep.* If you find you are not sleeping, or resting only fitfully, discuss this with your physician who may recommend an aid. *Most importantly—take only as much as prescribed.* A sympathetic therapist may be of help in talking through your emotions.

5. *Write* to them or about them. Write it in the form of a journey through your thoughts at this time or a letter to your child expressing how you miss them, but also remembering some light hearted, happy times.

6. *Relieving the tensions* of your mind and body when bereaving a loss is essential. Mental anguish can manifest itself into very real physical illness and, admit it, you are so vulnerable at this stage in your life. Have you noticed headaches, neck, shoulder, back and stomach pains? Any symptoms of ill health should be checked with a doctor. Also, here are some suggestions to aid yourself:

7. *Breathing:* Don't laugh, because we do this continually, automatically. I mean to have you breathe in *deeply*, through the nose, filling the lungs to capacity, hold for a second and release fully. Ten times a day when you remember can calm the mind and heart.

8. *Massage:* Head, neck and shoulders can work wonders and takes as short a time as 15-20 minutes, although enjoy for longer if you can! This is not an indulgence but good medicine.

9. *Yoga /Meditation /T'ai chi*

10. *Walking* or any other physical activity you enjoy. You don't have to train for a marathon.

11. *Change of scene.* Especially within the first six months, a change of environment can be a real help even if it's only two days away from home.

12. *Workplace.* Many people find that returning to the workplace is a help, since for a few hours there, the mind is resting from any pressing "home" decisions.

13. *Helping others* in some capacity means you will also help yourself within the involvement.

14. *Bereavement groups* are established to help by talking to others in similar situations and sharing ideas on moving onward through grief to a happier conclusion. It sounds strange to say "shop around" until you feel most comfortable in such a setting *or* form your own circle if you're so inclined, perhaps with a counselor for guidance.

15. *Accept help for yourself* whenever and in whatever way this is offered. You'd be surprised how many people find this to be difficult. It can be as simple as accepting a supper dish, an offer to grocery shop. Accept a lunch or dinner invitation or an offer to mow your lawn!

16. *Laughter.* Does this sound strange among your tears? Some of the best medicine is from laughter, which makes us fill our lungs with air and release muscle tension. You know that your beloved child would not want to see you continually despondent for them. *Smile* at the supermarket checkout person (they could be having difficulties, too). Smile at a child or that stranger walking toward you. You'll be happy to see how often they respond in kind! When you are perusing scenes of your child in the computer of your mind, tune in to one of those ridiculous moments and chuckle or laugh out loud at the memory. Rent a silly movie and laugh until you cry.

    The evening of our daughter's funeral service, we took her siblings and several of her friends to dinner. We began recounting stories about her and we were swiftly all engulfed in laughter, which continued throughout our time together. It was, without a doubt, one of the most hilarious, exhilarating and enjoyable evenings we have ever experienced and we are positive that Jenny was the instigator and shared every minute. Her sense of humor is one of the traits we recall so often.

17. *Start a Bereavement Scrapbook.* When you discover, or someone sends you, a particularly uplifting photograph, drawing, poem, article or other form of prose, save these in a scrapbook for those "blue" days when you need a little nudge into a positive frame of mind. A few minutes re-acquainting yourself with these pleasurable pages could provide the answer.

RELAXATION and MEDITATION.

    Throughout the grieving process we quite often hear, "you must relax"—"you need rest"—"your mind needs rest"—"quiet yourself." Easier said than done when the mind is re-running events and conversations like rewinding a video or it's "squirreling" around with details and questions and decisions to be made.

Some find it extremely difficult, almost impossible, to relax or sleep—especially in the first weeks of bereavement.

This is why we decided that we would give practical ways to achieve both states of relaxation and meditation with the hope that the explanation will further the healing processes.

RELAXATION.

SETTING.

Switch off telephones.

If daytime, subdue lighting by drawing curtains or pulling down shades, etc.

Remove shoes and any binding articles of clothing such as belts.

Lie down on a bed or sofa with the head, neck and shoulders supported by a pillow. (After a time you'll be able to just use the floor.)

For further comfort, some people like to have a small cushion or pillow under the knees.

READY to BEGIN.

For five *slow* counts take a deep breath—hold for one count—and completely expell for five counts.

Make an exaggerated *yawn*. Let the mouth drop gently open and wiggle the jaw from side-to-side. This begins to loosen the tension here.

Now squint the eyes tightly—"let go"—lids gently close.

Exaggerate another yawn. Keep jaw loose.

Tense / scrunch shoulders. "Let go."

Now we are ready to tense muscles and "let go" throughout the body.

With each tension take a deep breath to five counts—hold for one count—and as you empty the lungs to five counts, the muscles you are concentrating on will begin to relax.

You can begin with the feet or head, whichever is preferred, but repeat the above process with the :

> Shoulders
> Hands
> Stomach
> Thighs
> Calves

By the time you have *slowly* gone from head to toe or vice-versa you will have noticed some tension being released.

Eventually, you'll find that you no longer need to count to yourself but will simply *tense and unwind* slowly and naturally the more you practice.

Think of your head, neck and shoulders as sinking into the pillow. Your limbs and body drifting down through the bed / sofa / floor.

Breathe *deeply, steadily, slowly* through your nose. Exhale completely through relaxed lips.

Try this at night as you prepare to sleep.

Or

Perhaps for ten to fifteen minutes during the day.

The more you do this—the more skilled you become in *allowing* the tension to leave your body where it may have been contributing to your physical discomfort.

ONE MORE WORD: If it is at all possible—a head, neck and shoulder massage will absolutely aid immensely. In stressful situations, this is *not* an indulgent luxury but a nurturing healing.

NOW—float away on your own *special* cloud . . .

MEDITATION

Meditation is not some mysterious or "New Age" ritual but a

very ancient practice that enables the inner quietness and peaceful solitude of mind to be reached.

The total suspension of mind for five, ten, fifteen minutes or longer, according to preference, can renew and refresh both physically and mentally.

Meditation is something which can be done anywhere, anytime for a moment of peace and calm.

It can be done in the office, on a bus or train, sitting on a park bench, at home in the morning or last thing at night, however needed and practiced uninterrupted.

SETTING.

Switch off telephones.
Subdue lighting.
Softly played music or gentle nature sounds.
Silence.
Perfumed candles. (Some find this contributes to the ambience of peace.)

READY to BEGIN.

Sit or lie comfortably.
Take a deep breath through the nose while *slowly* counting silently to five, hold for one count, then release through partially open mouth.

Continue to breathe *slowly, gently*—filling the lungs to capacity in this way before releasing.

Close eyes if desired or concentrate on an object before you.

Continue breathing quietly while from the top of the head *imagine* any tension being released and flowing *down* and *out* through the neck and *dropping off* the shoulders.

With the next breath, the throat relaxes as the *thought-flow* takes tension away from that area and the chest.

Feel the arms and hands ease and be limp.

Stomach releases.

Hips and lower back respond to the tension continuing to leave the body with each exhalation of breath.

Legs and feet "sink" earthward.

Let all thought drift away and enjoy the total relaxation of mind and body with the next breaths.

Breath in the *Silence* and *Peace* of the moment.

VISUALIZATION.

It is at this contented and restful stage that some visualize or *see* within the *mind's eye* a place of sanctuary to which the mind seeks to *visit* at each meditation.

This *place* may be a room . . . .

A garden . . .

A beach . . .

Or mountains . . . .

A beautiful place actually visited or one imagined.

In this solitude and peaceful enjoyment, some discover the answer to a perplexing question or simply immerse the self into stressless moments.

RETURNING.

When ready to emerge from a meditation—do so *slowly*.

The heart-rate will have slowed through experiencing the calmness.

As awareness of actual surroundings occur, *gently stir* the body and limbs.

Take a final cleansing breath, and feel *refreshed*.

There are helpful books and interesting guided meditations on audiotapes which can be borrowed from public libraries as well as purchased from any bookstore.

Your Thoughts

CHAPTER 12

BIRTHDAYS & SEASONAL OBSERVANCES

Dear Friend:

One of the most difficult questions you will face in the first year following your child's death is their birthday and the anniversary of their passing.

What to do?

Shall I observe the dates?

How shall I live through those reminders that my child is with us no longer?

Once more, as you have noticed on this experience that our minds, hearts and souls have been thrust into, it is a decision, a choice to be made solely by *you*.

1. You may want to simply light a special candle.

Or you may be comfortable in:

2. Setting a place at the dinner table and remembering other birthdays. While this can be a comfort to some families, other parents find it a too poignant reminder of a chair never to be used by their person again.

3. Preparing a favorite meal and raising a glass in happy memory as their journey continues.
4. Inviting two or three of their friends to a place of special significance to your child, giving them a chance to remember, also.
5. Providing flowers at your place of worship and having prayers and/or a blessing for the beloved.

On the other hand, some parents feel that they need to be quite alone with their thoughts and even make a point of taking a few days away from the home environment. Do whatever feels best for *you.*

It is a difficult time, no doubt about it, but I promise you that it becomes less stressful after the first year.

Now what of those other seasonal observances?

Most definitely they will never be the same.

You are going to have to make other changes which, eventually, become family traditions.

But that first year will be *difficult*—with the advertisements showing happy, smiling, "perfect" families. Decorations seemingly everywhere. Everyone cheerful.

You want to scream out to the world, "Stop! How *dare* you laugh and plan parties and enjoy yourselves? Don't you know that my child can't do that?"

This is also a time when some families will travel to a totally different environment.

But what if that is impractical or impossible?

There are suggestions for the gift-giving time and we have done this since the first year of our daughter's demise for her birthdays, both heavenly and earthly, plus at Christmas.

Whatever amount you would have spent, use that money in their memory to purchase and donate to:

1. Books to a library or school.
2. A Teen Outreach program.

3. A charity in which your person was particularly interested (for animals or people).
4. Planting a sapling or a flowering bush in a local park or garden.

There will always be a few tears no matter what we decide to do for their observances but they will become happier tears as the years continue and our memories become more light-hearted in acceptance of their continued journeys.

CHAPTER 13

PROMISES #2

We, Jenny's father and I, would like to express our sincerest, deepest sympathy to everyone who has experienced the passing of a beloved child because of substances of any kind.

One thing is for certain. We will *never* stop loving these souls who have departed. They continue to be a part of our lives as we think of them, share memories with others as well as ourselves.

These are our very special people who also came into our lives to be cherished and will have left us with some special gifts of learning.

We each have our own unique circumstances and yet we are brought together through a common thread—a bond.

No—*you are not alone.* We are here.

There is no time limit on grief and moving through it.

You'll certainly learn more because of this experience.

And, *this I promise you:* You *will* smile, laugh, and savor life again. In fact, you may treasure life more.

To hope, to know, to feel that our children *are at last* at peace from their torments and are truly well and happy, isn't that what we wish for them?

Happiness and wellness be with each and every one of us.

"Perhaps they are not the stars
But rather openings in Heaven
Where the love of our lost ones
Pours through and shines down
Upon us to let us know they are happy."

(Inspired by an Eskimo legend, author unknown.)

CHAPTER 14

HOW CAN I HELP SOMEONE WHOSE CHILD HAS DIED?

Do say: "I am sorry." "I am sad for your loss."
Do offer to: Grocery shop.

Pick up dry cleaning.

Take a meal ready to pop into the microwave or oven.

Telephone to say a brief "hello."

Listen.

Have a shoulder to cry on—an arm to hold them.

Take the parents out for a meal whenever they feel ready to do so.

Instead of flowers at a service, offer a plant, shrub or tree to be planted in the deceased's name, or make a donation to a charitable organization that may have been an interest of the deceased.

If there are younger children:

Take them to an activity they enjoy.

Take them out to lunch.

Take or pick them up from school.

Listen the *their* concerns.

Be there—but only say it if that is true.

Send a plant for the family.
Listen to what your heart says to do to comfort. Hold.
Mention the deceased.
Weep. Share.

Bereavement Scrapbook: In Chapter 11, regarding the next step forward—"Things To Do"—I have mentioned the scrapbook. This is something a friend could begin for someone in grief. You can title this book in a creative way and fill it with anything uplifting such as photographs, drawings, poems, articles, sayings, etc.

The idea behind this book is for it to offer a little sunlight on the gray, cloudy days that can strike at any time. Does this sound too simple? It is often the simplest, loving thoughts and deeds that are most appreciated.

Do NOT:

Do *not* say, "I understand" *or* "I know exactly how you are feeling." You do *not* know. You cannot know. Unless you have been there yourself. This is a uniquely personal occurrence for each individual person.

Do *not* say, "If this happened to my child, I'd . . ." Well—it *hasn't* happened and, at this moment in time, to be quite honest with you, we don't want to know about your happy, fortunate, *living* child. Go home and hold your child close.

Do *not* say, "Perhaps if he/she had attended a church . . . ." Perhaps this child was as spiritual as one in an organized religious group. Addictions know no boundaries.

Do *not* say, "We had our pet dog/cat for 15 years and it was just like losing a child." How can anyone compare an animal to a child, a human soul made out of love, nurtured and laughed with, worried and prayed over? (You'd be surprised how many people really do say this, intending somehow to offer comfort!)

Do *not* relay success stories of recovery from addictions of your children, nephews, and nieces. All parents, too, wanted with all their heart to see their daughter or son in the career of their choice, leading a healthy life-style, married, perhaps with children of their own.

And DO NOT inform parents of new treatments guaranteed to cure addictions. These cures are all too late for their children.

Oh, yes, in time parents shall be happy for other children and to learn of new treatments for this terrible thing called addiction, but just now, to be honest, there is resentment at observing carefree youth. They are *alive* and ours are dead.

And, please, do not mention divorce in the context of grief.

Yes, divorce can be painfully uprooting but the two *adult* partners have made that choice and their lives will continue and eventually, perhaps, end on a "happily ever after" note.

The finality of death has nothing in comparison with a divorce. There are no choices to be made.

Your Thoughts

CHAPTER 15

"PLEASE"

Here is a wonderful poem that embodies a parent's emotions and thoughts on this most gut wrenching of tragedies. It was sent to me from a mother whose son had also overdosed and died from heroin. We couldn't discover the author and print it here now with my "answers and comments" to each verse.

PLEASE

"Please don't ask me if I'm over it yet."
I'll never be over it.

Each day I will miss my child until I, too, die. I may not cry as often or hurt as much, but my soul will always have a missing piece.

"Please don't tell me she's in a better place."
She's not here with me.

Afterlife may be all we've been told it is but my child's place is here living this life and in my arms.

"Please don't say at least she's not suffering."
I haven't come to terms why she had to suffer at all.

She and we battled so much to overcome the demons of addictions. The "why" questions will always be there. Why did she? Why God?

"Please don't ask me if I feel better."
Bereavement isn't a condition that clears up.

It would be so very nice if all the heartache could pass away as quickly as a cold. It takes time.

"Please don't tell me you know how I feel unless you
have lost your daughter."

Losing a child is far from the demise of a parent, a sibling or friend. However close we were to these people we cannot know them as deeply as that being we birthed, nurtured and for whom we had dreams and hopes of the future.

"Please don't tell me, 'At least you had her for so
many years.' What year would *you* choose for your
daughter to die?"

We actually thought of this when we saw toys at gravesites of babies. Is it somehow less painful not to have watched her develop, walk, talk, or explore life? No age, year or time is the right time. Whatever the allotted years, it is never enough.

"Please don't tell me God never gives us
more than we can bear."

Because right now I am breaking up into little pieces from the physical and mental anguish, the pain of this loss, and I doubt very sincerely whether I'll be able to "bear" this experience.

"Please just say you're sorry."
Please just say you remember my daughter, if you do.

I appreciate simple statements from the heart. And I rejoice in your sharing a memory of my child.

> "Please just let me talk about my daughter.
> Please mention my daughter's name."

Don't you know that everything reminds me of my daughter? A song, a flower, a place. Her essence touched all that is around me. I love to hear her name. There are endless happy moments I can tell you about that will let you know the wonderful person my daughter really was and is.

> "Please just let me cry."

Her name or thoughts may bring tears but these tears are healing for me. I don't mind if you turn away in embarrassment but, please, let me cry because I need to think of my feelings, not yours.

"Speak to us of Children"
"You may give them your love but not your thoughts,
For they have their own thoughts.
You may house their bodies but not their souls,
For their souls dwell in the house of tomorrow."

"The Prophet"—Kahlil Gibran

CHAPTER 16

ADDICTIONS & CHOICE

Dear Friend,

Many books have been written and there are varied opinions on the subject of addictions. I shall leave the arguments to the experts.

Opinions expressed here are our own learning experiences through living with our daughter Jenny and, also, talking with other parents.

For sure, those of us who have never been caught up into the insidious web of substance addictions, whether alcohol or any other drug, can only guess at the physical and mental miseries these unfortunate souls have to battle.

Many people will say that it's a matter of choice. So it is, *in the beginning.*

Usually it is someone else's choice: Pressure from a peer or others to just *"try* this beer, wine, marijuana, or ecstasy."

This triggers sensors in the pleasure points of the brain and the next choice to repeat a sensation is the person who had been urged to *"try—just once."*

Then follows a more frequent desire for whatever substance answers the brain's call; after which it is so easy—no effort at all—to slide down the slippery slope into an every day craving of the addict.

At this point even the physical body has to be satisfied or it cries out in spasms of pain in many ways.

Choice here? No. All self-choice has gone, to be replaced by the demands of the drugs or alcohol.

But what of the person who is not an addict? What of the person who had tried a pill, some other substance or been urged to drink too much at the one and only time?

That is one of the most frightening aspects of these scenarios. *We do not know* why some bodies have one jolt and shut down rapidly in protest.

Another person can use once, decide "never again," and stop.

Yet another can be drinking and misusing and realize that they are in serious trouble with their mind and body, can work with treatments and survive.

Then we have the drugs or alcoholic addict who tries time after time, treatment after treatment and cannot, with all their efforts, release themselves from this grip of hell.

Sooner or later only death brings relief for them.

We still do not have the answer to "why?"

When we speak of addictions to young people we stress this truth upon them because the awful reality is that no one knows into which category they belong and all youth believe they are invincible. They will never die in this way.

For many, many people addictions are a disease. It is a poisonous disease without an antidote.

That is the true tragedy and shame.

Shame as in "such a pity," a sorrow.

And survivors are left with the tears, the sorrow.

Our daughter believed that, one day, researchers would discover that gene which would tell by testing whose DNA carried the spore of addictions, so that babies would be tested while yet in the womb or shortly after birth to eliminate the defect.

There are so many answers being found daily that I really would hope we could save future generations from the agonies that our sick children endured. Thus, also, relieving the frustrating searches, nightmares and heartaches that parents and others have had to live through.

Your Thoughts

CHAPTER 17

FREQUENTLY ASKED QUESTIONS

As with all bereavement—loss of any kind—no one can predict a "time-line," a beginning and an end. Neither should we, since grief and recovery vary from individual to individual and has to be concluded by that person.

When a death occurs, however, there are questions we hear over and over again. We offer some answers here based on our own and others' experiences.

Q. How long does the pain of loss last? My child died six months ago and there are days when I still have physical pain.

> A. Physical pain is one of the manifestations of bereavement, which some people experience and no one can say in what duration of time it will "disappear." Grief can make our heart actually feel as though it is "broken." Sometimes this pain can affect digestion. After checking with a physician to be sure there is no actual, physical reason for pain, learning to relax may help. But do not be surprised if twinges of pain return occasionally over the next months or even the first year.

Q. When we had the service I did not cry. I am sure that my lack of tears caused some people to question my behavior. What is wrong with me?

A. First of all, there is nothing *wrong* with you. In the privacy of your home, the tears have probably flowed. Quite often by the day of the service, we respond on "automatic pilot." This is because we mistakenly feel we must put on a "public face" and not make others feel uncomfortable. Nonsense. Both these are foolish thoughts!

Q. Sometimes I suddenly find myself in tears in a department store or the supermarket. Am I normal?

A. What is normal? Of course, you're *normal*. You have experienced and are continuing to be in the throes of a tremendously traumatic time. Especially in the first year, a sudden image or thought of your person can flash into your mind and it's overwhelming! Simply leave the store (even in the middle of a purchase). Sit in your car to cry and recover before driving home.

Q. I cannot bear to hear or say the word "dead" about my loss.

A. The word is synonymous with finality. The finality of life with this person, no matter how it has been (and there must have been good times as well as bad). Death has the sting of taboo connected with it in the Western world and we never really discuss or dwell upon it. This is why with GRASP (see page 97) it was decided to generally use the word "passing" in deference to you and others who feel this way. With time, you will feel easier about the word but in the beginning of bereaving, it is a way of denying the end of one experience or episode of your life.

Q. Why do I feel as though I need permission to laugh again?

A. Could it be because of grieving being portrayed as continuous "weeping and wailing?" You see yourself as being judged by an outside world. We don't want to appear disrespectful to the one who has gone. And yet, would they really want you to remain sad and tearful? Laughter and smiles are some of the best medicine for us. After our daughter's service, as mentioned in Chapter 11, we had a marvelous dinner with her siblings and best friends during which someone remarked about a humorous incident they had had with her and that began a most wonderful meal of sharing, laughing and loving together. We really felt her presence joining in with us. There was no time for weeping and wailing.

Q. What should I do about possessions?

A. This is such a personal decision and not one to be hurried. You should decide about possessions only when you are absolutely ready to sort and pack and, perhaps, share items with others. This does not have to be accomplished in one day, or week, or month. Do it in your time frame.

Q. What is it with my other kids? They don't talk about their brother. Don't they care?

A. More often than you can imagine, we hear this question and, of course, you know the siblings *are* grieving, too. There are several reasons why you feel they are not being as responsive as you would want or even expect them to behave, depending on their ages.

Young children appear to cope, accept and continue their usual routine of life after perhaps an initial puzzlement of this phenomena of death. They may or may not cry. Encourage them to share their thoughts with drawings or writing a letter to the departed one. There also are some excellent books for youngsters.

Older siblings often hesitate to confide their grief to you for fear of upsetting you further if and when you outwardly *appear* to be coping. Perhaps they do not know how to manage their grief, which may be tinged with anger or resentment. Anger at the person for causing this pain for you and the rest of the family. Resentment of the time already devoted to the departed person in trying to help them, and now, even in death, continuing to be the major focus of home life.

There is anger and confusion within themselves for even thinking this way. It is as if they almost need your "permission" to talk about them with you.

By your willingness to voice your hurt at this time, and in so doing reveal how you are perceiving their attitudes, you open a door to everyone's emotions, and as you verbalize such feelings, it becomes an opportunity to discuss your departed child.

Don't let their responses or non-responsiveness keep you from talking about, and enjoying, incidents in your late child's life.

Q. When will I be my "old self" again, as friends expect me to be eventually? They say things like, "Take it easy and you'll soon get right back on track."

A. Accept that you are never going to be exactly your "old self" again. You're going to be making changes in routines, adjusting almost daily to continuing life with a treasured piece of human fabric missing. You may even change how you have always looked at and thought about this earthly life. You will be learning about *a new* you, and who's to say this isn't better than the *old* you?

CHAPTER 18

POEMS

I have included the following poems because they give a voice to our departed children. Many of our children were multi-talented in the arts and left us wonderful gifts of paintings, drawings, prose and poetry.

In a meditation one day, approximately two years after our daughter's demise, this verse repeated itself in the semiconsciousness. I know it is from her.

> All that I should have been
> All that I could have been
> Here—
> I am.

Here is another poem by Jenny:

In the Beyond
I long
To hold you, too.
To be able to speak out loud
To have you hear.
Do not weep.
I know you can feel me near.

In the Beyond
I work with you
And learn
And maybe
I will learn to reach
To touch
To speak
All is possible

Though we miss you all
As you miss us
We can be happy together
Because we are close—
So very close.

———————————————

This last was written with inspiration from Jason:
11/26/74- 4/11/99.

In The Silence.

In the Silence, mom, you hear me
In the Silence, I am here.
In the Silence, you can feel me
In the Silence it is clear
That my spirit hasn't left you,
I am just a thought away.

You can see me in the shadows
Anytime you look my way.
Look for me in the sunshine
And in the stars at night.
In the wind, trees and flowers,
Everything that is in sight.

Talk to me, say my name.
Know that I'm still here.
In my death I have a new life
And one day it will be clear.
So talk to me and look for me
In everything you do
For I haven't gone so far away
I'm really right next to you.

CHAPTER 19

DREAMS

"For life and death are one,
even as the river and sea are one.
In the depth of your hopes and desires lies
your secret knowledge of the beyond.
Trust the dreams, for in them is
hidden the gate to eternity."

"The Prophet"—Kahlil Gibran

Shortly after talking with bereaved families or communicating with them through the Internet, we heard from people, hesitantly at first, who confided that they experienced dreams concerning the deceased.

Describing the dreams is difficult, not because of content, but because of the *emotion* experienced during this state and continuing afterward.

"You're going to think I'm crazy, but—" is often expressed.

"It's unlike any dream I've ever had before."

"It's so real."

"I know I was there."

"I know he/she was really here"

The vivid experience of a "visit" to the bedroom by their beloved young person or meeting them somewhere.

Sensing the communication and message without actually speaking.

Conversing with one another.

Embracing.

Knowing the special smell of the person.

These dreams occur shortly after death. After the funeral or memorial service, or weeks or even months later. In other words, at no particular time and quite unexpectedly.

They seem to happen once or many times for some people. There is no set pattern.

Others ask us why they have never experienced this sort of communication when they hear of these dreams.

Of course, we cannot really answer that question since we do not know why or how this is manifest.

Yes, we understand that the medical communities insist it is because we, in our intense grief, fulfill our need to know that our children (and others) are free of pain and are happy. In other words, we manufacture our dreams just as we can dream of an incident after viewing a movie or reading.

However, the argument against this is wrought from the waking state.

Most dreams are forgotten immediately upon waking or, if remembered, we cannot recall minute details.

With the special dreams we are discussing here, there is definite memory, not only of the person, but surroundings, color, any conversation, and, most important, *emotions* experienced during and after.

Sometimes there are sadness and tears, which are quickly overcome at parting once more, but most often, we are left with an overwhelming sense of love, joy and peace.

It is an indescribable feeling of a love so pure in its essence that it calms the very soul.

Experiences of this nature are *never* forgotten no matter how many years lapse between the recalling of them.

No, we haven't an explanation for you and, perhaps, we are not supposed to know since there are many happenstances in this world for which even the finest minds cannot offer answers.

As we were asked by one father and mother, how could they have had absolutely *identical* dreams of their child on the same night and at the same time and awoke to tell one another?

Jennifer's last visitation with me was several years ago now while Russ and I were staying at a cousin's home in England.

My daughter and I had "spent some time together" in joyous silent conversation, which was the way of our dream communications. Suddenly Jennifer said aloud, "I have to go now."

As I heard those words, I *knew* within my being that it meant I might not see her this way again.

"Oh, no," I pleaded.

Jennifer opened her arms and for the *first* time in these dreamlike meetings we could hold one another. I *actually felt* her precious body, smelled the essence of her as we clung.

"Don't worry, mummy," she murmured soothingly. "It's okay. I'll be back. I'm coming back."

She rose from the bench on which we were sitting and slowly disappeared as she walked away, never looking back.

The pain seared my heart as much as on first hearing of our loss and I was wracked with deep sobs, the sounds of which I tried to muffle so as not to awaken anyone.

But as I failed to stifle the noise, I reached out for Russ who quietly gathered me into his arms, stroking my head until the emotion subsided.

Unlike previous communications, I was not able to tell him what had transpired for several hours. He understood. He is ever my comforter.

We can tell you this. If you experience unusually lifelike dreams of your departed, you are *not* peculiar or crazy in any way whatsoever. Just *welcome* to the rest of us!

Your Thoughts

CONCLUSION

So, dear friend, we have come this far together. I hope by sharing these thoughts that you have discovered whatever help or answers you were seeking and that this little book will continue to aid you during future months.

Some of you may have been asking yourselves, "How did Pat and Russ get from there to here? What did they do to find peace of heart?"

We realize, of course, that we have been blessed with a strong bond of love between us. So many times in such situations, marriages will crumble.

The first year after our daughter's demise was the worst of our lives, no doubt about it. Then, slowly, quietly, almost without realizing it, calmness was replacing the anxious and hurting soul.

Almost from the beginning, we felt a need to make sense of this senseless situation.

We had established a memorial fund in her name to help young people rescued from a street-life, especially those with substance problems. We needed to do more.

The germ of an idea festered in my brain. But how to begin?

I sat down at my desk with paper and pen ready. I prayed. I sought guidance through God and asked for Jenny's help, also.

The title came. I wrote it down. We had begun.

"Jenny's Journey."

The complete presentation—I *knew* I was to use these words in schools to reach the youth—was written that day. In segments. In simple language. Six photographs were enlarged to giant poster size, including one of Jenny in her casket, which was to be most important to audiences. After searching through home movies, I had a five-minute "clip" compiled professionally.

The need was to show that this young woman was an ordinary person like any other who came from a caring home. Junkies aren't necessarily "the dregs" as society would like to believe. Jenny would be the face for drug addiction.

The first presentation was held one evening for our church members, who packed the building. The second presentation was for youth in a residential treatment facility, and the third, for a middle school with PTA representatives as part of the audience.

Since then "Jenny's Journey" has been overwhelmingly accepted and encouraged by:

> Elementary, middle and high schools.
> Technical colleges.
> Residential substance facilities.
> Recovering addicts programs.
> Youth drug court programs.
> Foster parents and other public groups.
> Social services programs.

A video was professionally produced in both 15 and 30 minute versions, together with a comprehensive facilitator's study guide. These are used in schools and elsewhere.

Through talking about Jenny, Pat and Russ found that total strangers were coming to share their *sometimes secret* family's experiences of drugs and death.

As a result, G.R.A.S.P. (*Grief Recovery After a Substance Passing*) was an idea, a concept discussed and decided upon.

It took some time for GRASP to be *conceived and born*, although a minister friend had suggested that we reach out to others in this way.

When we met with our first couple of bereaved parents, we realized other truths:

You do not need a degree to listen, to comfort—to share.

You *do* need to have experienced the pain of struggling before this tragic happening.

Oh, one more thing before we leave you. A question for you, friend. Think about this:

> When we lose a spouse, we are widowed.
> When we lose parents, we are orphaned.
> When we lose a child, we are—?
> There isn't a word or name for us. Isn't it strange?

Your Thoughts

G.R.A.S.P.

GRIEF RECOVERY AFTER A
SUBSTANCE PASSING

Judy was the last to leave that Saturday's monthly get-together in the Carriage House of the church. For several hours, eight members of our group had been exchanging stories, all dealing with the personal loss of a child through substance misuse, either drugs or alcohol.

With everyone sharing a similar bond, there has always been a refreshing frankness to be shared. We had long since realized that *only* if you have personally experienced the loss of a child through drugs, can one fully appreciate the depths of emotions that particular loss brings.

At each meeting, there is help from one to another, shared experiences, and a promise of continuing support in whatever way each of us can contribute to the others.

Judy had lost her 21-year-old daughter just a year before, through alcohol, and is still trying to sort out answers. This was her third GRASP meeting.

She left for only a moment. Then we heard a gentle rap on the door. It opened and Judy looked in and said, "I just wanted to let you know, I really appreciate that you are there for me."

A simple incident, but it encompasses the reasons we knew we had to start GRASP several years ago. People who have lost a child through drugs are in great need of help, but especially from people who have been there.

We've found that, as helpful as the written word may be, it is the *in-person* contact between like-grieving people that provides the most benefit.

GRASP meets once a month, and each month there are returnees and, often, new people who have found no source for their particular kind of grief, and then somehow have heard about us. Meetings are really just "get-togethers," opportunities to share coffee, refreshments, and experiences.

We feel the true benefit of this book and of GRASP is to encourage people everywhere to start their own GRASP groups. The more person-to-person contact there is between people with like hurts and real needs, the better we will serve those who now feel they are some sort of reprehensible lost souls.

If you'd like our suggestions and input on our experiences in starting GRASP in San Diego, we will be happy to share.

CONTACT PAT AND RUSS

The Wittbergers are parents of six children, have six grandchildren and find it difficult to realize they are also *great*-grandparents.

Russ is a Milwaukee native and a graduate of Marquette University's College of Journalism. He recently retired as director of marketing for Metro Networks following a 25-year career in broadcast management.

Pat, formerly a professional actress and dancer, wrote the scripts for the "Jenny's Journey" drug misuse presentations and video and has contributed an article to the Naval magazine, "Ashore." She wrote several chapters about their daughter Jennifer, which will appear in a book by British journalist Fiona Griffiths.

Pat and Russ encourage you to be in touch with them for your thoughts on this book, to formulate a GRASP group or simply to say "hello." They can be reached through their websites (following) or even regular mail.

www.jennysjourney.org
www.grasphelp.org

62 Holly Ribbons Circle
Bluffton,
South Carolina 29909
USA

All proceeds from the sale of this book help continue the outreach programs of "Jenny's Journey" and G.R.A.S.P. (Grief Recovery After a Substance Passing).

Do not stand at my grave and weep.
I am not there. I do not sleep.
I am a thousand winds that blow.
I am the diamond glints on snow.
I am the sunlight on ripened grain.
I am the gentle autumn rain.
When you awaken in the morning's rush,
I am the swift, uplifting rush
Of quiet birds in circling flight.
I am the soft star that shines at night.
Do not stand at my grave and cry.
I am not there.
I did not die.

Anonymous

Personal Thoughts

13965190R00062